SHIFT

Phoenix·Poets

A SERIES EDITED BY ALAN SHAPIRO

shift

JEREDITH MERRIN

THE UNIVERSITY OF CHICAGO PRESS *Chicago & London*

Jeredith Merrin is associate professor of English at the Ohio State University. She is the author of *An Enabling Humility* (1990), a study of Marianne Moore and Elizabeth Bishop.

The University of Chicago Press, Chicago 60637
The University of Chicago Press, Ltd., London
© 1996 by The University of Chicago
All rights reserved. Published 1996
Printed in the United States of America

05 04 03 02 01 00 99 98 97 96   1 2 3 4 5

ISBN 0-226-52063-3 (cloth)
ISBN 0-226-52064-1 (paper)

Library of Congress Cataloging-in-Publication Data

Merrin, Jeredith, 1944–
    Shift /Jeredith Merrin.
        p.   cm. — (Phoenix poets)
    1. Lesbians—Poetry. 2. Love poetry, American. I. Title.   II. Series.
PS3563.E745333S55   1996
811´.54—dc20   95-39347
                                                CIP

∞ The paper used in this publication meets the minimum requirements of the American National Standard for Information Sciences—Permanence of Paper for Printed Library Materials, ANSI Z39.48-1984.

for Diane Furtney

Contents

Acknowledgments

Grateful acknowledgment is made to the following publications in which these poems first appeared:

Agni: "Blue Skies," "Sublunar"
Bay Windows: "Shift"
Berkeley Poetry Review: "Summer before College," "To Gram at Ninety"
Kenyon Review: "Fourth and Main"
MS.: "Journal Entry, WordPerfect 5.1"
Nebo: "From the Rooftops"
Occident: "Divorce, a Letter to Canada," "The Lineaments of Gratified Desire," "Moving"
Paris Review: "Dream-View of Delft," "The Shadow Plant"
Ploughshares: "Grieving"
Poetry Northwest: "Lisa, Reading"
San Jose Studies: "End of Summer," "Opening Up"
Threepenny Review: "Mutual Attraction," "The Right Words"
Yale Review: "Big Sister"

"Summer before College" was reprinted in *Diamonds Are a Girl's Best Friend: Women Writers on Baseball,* ed. Elinor Nauen (Boston: Faber and Faber, 1994).

Special thanks to Robert Pinsky, Alfred Corn, Irving Feldman, and Louise Glück for commenting on earlier versions of the manuscript. I wish also to thank the Ragdale Foundation for offering two residencies, and Helen Deutsch for her friendship and encouragement over the years.

MUTUAL ATTRACTION   **o n e**

for Diane

Opening Up

Tulips, doors, thighs, of course,
and so on—the predictable vistas
of music, mirrors, and other surfaces
that might disclose suddenly
my own startled face,
are what I think of;
also, an elm on an ample estate,
offering its vase of limbs
at the end of the several
greens of imposing grounds;

the terrible holes of sharks'
mouths, and closets,
and occasional bad dreams;
roses, too, in time-lapse photography
toward an old age and death
by fits and starts, their moths
of blossoms extending
thoughtlessly, and then it's all over.

And I think of what I never noticed,
the incessant constellations,
and more: rooms where we left
each door and window open,
how the moon made a pale spot
on one focal wall,

so that I finally saw through
to what else was possible—the rain
sounding on the low roof
like a sheet of canvas tearing,
as if some titan had imagined,
unfolded, and pitched the huge tent
now being slowly ripped
open over our heads.

Shift

How can
I describe a conversion
like this one?

A massive shifting,
as of plates rearranging
along a continental shelf, causing

slight tremors? Maybe.
There are forces we don't see,
a subterranean geography.

Or something like a change
of season—the strange
but ordinary way trees rearrange

shape and color,
standing in the same places? Her
love was neither cure-

all nor catastrophe; not, in lieu
of the usual, a compromise. Go where you
will, do

what you can. As for me,
the scales tipped when she
touched me, just lightly.

End of Summer

Berkeley, 1985

Under your high window's brandy light
our tousled bed's transformed:
the gold sails we admired
in the Dutch print on your wall
have again become our sheets;
the bed our *bateau ivre*;
about us, water.

It took me half my life, or more, to get here.

Summer, like this day, is almost over.
I see her stoop to gather
with a little shiver
her flimsy yellow shawl
—the landscape's scattered lights—
then wrap herself, stand tall,
and start away.

Mutual Attraction

A secretive girl, she got those scars
breaking into houses. Nights, she clambers
up rough siding, wedges between
half-opened windows, spills over cluttered
piano tops. Groping in musty rugs,
creeping across parquet, linoleum, what is
she searching for with her white, long fingers,
while you lie dreaming of one yellow apple
up high on a well-picked tree? You think
you can, think you can . . .

Now the moon is a rabbit, an egg, one eye
of a black cat, winking; the triform
goddess—Luna, Diana, Proserpina—in all
of the three worlds, searching.

Or a brain, preserved, floating
in that inky fluid, and still
thinking: *How beautiful she looks,*
the blue Earth, my body—her seas
still pulsing because I remember them
(though my own—Serenitas,
Nectaris, Imbrium—are only ashes);
how she tingles with life. I imagine
when she sleeps I stroke her, hold her
for hours in my phantom arms.

Meanwhile, your body vaguely aches
in its sleep, and you vow to hang on
through all her changes—hoofprint,
huge white bird, unsounded gong—
to keep her forever in your own arms.

"The Lineaments of Gratified Desire"

Lost, finally, to the world
of suffering and ambition,
humiliation and conquest—
all the battle din passed
far over the hill now,
the massed red and yellow banners,
the racket of lances . . .

I remember the thunder of horses,
a churning as they crossed the broad noon river.

Here, though, is no clangor, no armor.

The proof may be close by
that the world is the world still.

But I am not in it;
I have fought to lose it.
And the tears you see signal
no discord or sadness.
The muscular horses long ago crossed over
bearing splendid, wrackful battalions,
leaving behind them this river of silver.

From the Rooftops

From rooftops tiled with squared-off,
military, slate-gray waves,
or with rose petals
(in curvature and color)
of the Spanish variety,

down to the quiet corner
where a red cat in a serious campaign
stalks an insect or bird,
and the bougainvillea clambers to heaven
on its mustard-colored wall,

how full and notable this small town,
Berkeley, seems, replete with epic themes
of love and war. Even the trees
are various and inexhaustible,
not unlike some prodigious

vocabulary: the redwood, linden,
sweetgum, sycamore, flowering
mimosa, eucalyptus, ginko, elm.
And this noticing of abundance
follows somehow from our love—

the battle we engage in cheerfully
against a few limited others

and the less praiseworthy
parts of ourselves.
How grateful I am for it;

for you, now, when sunlight
on the wild grass in the lot
down there (I'm sitting, sunning
on my own apartment roof) recalls
you, fierce and luminous,

and the bright hair
you habitually and casually flick
(revising your copious poems)
from your white brow. Behind
that brow, that mind.

BLACKMAIL

t w o

for my stepfather

The Best Cook

In the open-air restaurant, a woman
at the next table turns to an impatient child,
possibly her granddaughter, and says:

"I *know* you're hungry. Hunger is the best cook,
my mother always said." And I didn't think then
of the starving in Africa or the hungry-eyed,

angry veteran without arms or legs I see often
and pass quickly on a sidewalk in Berkeley, who steers
his wheeled table by holding in his mouth a sort of metal straw.

I thought instead of that well-fed woman's mother
and of my stepfather, a Polish Jew, dead last year.
He had emigrated before the War, working

odd jobs as a busboy, milkman, and part-time cantor;
then a chemist, Hebrew teacher, Hebrew school director—
finally retiring to Israel where a Jew could be

"in full power and proud." His last summer, every week
two or three of his students came to visit, asking
his advice—all grateful that he'd "changed my life."

I sat beside him on that balcony
in Jerusalem—a single mother, myself
by then a teacher, but still hungry for his

never-spoken "I love you." "I'm so lonely," I sobbed.
"Everyone is lonely," he said, fat and impassive.
"It's the human condition." Across the bay,

pollarded sycamores with their flailing arms
and fists stand outside the squat, domed City Hall
with its heavy carved doors. Farther out, west, are rows

of slender pastel houses—powder-blue, gold,
cream and peach—lined up and naively expectant
as girls at a dance. In the tender sunset light,

their fire escapes are sashes and their large windows
shine. The orange pendent bridge keeps reaching, yearning,
and everyone, it's the human condition, is hungry.

Grieving

I want to do this right,
as though there were a right way
of walking or sitting still,
of staring at stoplights changing—
even a right way to smoke,
to hold a cup.

I remember after surgery
when the pain was intense,
I thought there must be a right way
to walk through its bright mazes—
curious, but unimpressed.

All vanity, that self-consciousness,
I think he would say: the fox
gnawing its foot off in a trap,
the cat bearing a difficult litter,
suffer without drama.

I've heard, though, of elephants
that grieve: a cow nudges
a stillborn calf, or maybe
lingers over a motionless bull.

Whether or not they really ponder
as they seem to,
I imagine one, anxious,
urging, "Get up! Get up!"—
but silent, somehow
without self-interest.

Moving

I expected this, the way
everything suddenly has scent and color
because it is the first time,
and the old desire reasserts itself—
like the violet of that just-noticed
wall rising from wet pavement—
the desire to be more,
while there's still time.
But in this new city,
each fresh sensation is familiar
as the cigarette smell
just passed on my walk; is thin
as a blond girl's skin,
almost transparently covering
her small bones—and it rubs off
too quickly, like the cordovan
finish of the shoes I scuffed
racing home from second grade
in September. This fall,
underneath is your death.
Nearing my new apartment,
I hear you just behind me,
though you so carefully imitate
my own measured pace.

The Right Words

Summers, in staggered sizes,
we got into the Dodge
and the man we called Father drove

up or down the coast.
The youngest, shy, nearsighted,
secretly violent, what I liked

was the smack of waves on rocks;
tidepools where anemones snatched
with curled and restless fingers

small fish glittering
like pennies, nickels,
or like the right words

in fairy tales—the charms
that fill an empty bowl
or keep the terrible big trolls

away from Boots. One night,
Father put my goldfish
in an ashtray, showing me

it couldn't breathe
in air. I didn't want
the lesson about gills and screamed

to put it back, watching it thrash
and thrash before he would,
while nothing I said worked.

Now, after typing for hours,
striking with restless fingers,
I step outside: sun softens

the propriety of brick
and falls in yellow oblong
patches on the grass,

inviting as lit windows
on a cold night's walk.
Not far away, in warmth

behind the thin glass,
are wished-for moments
and the words that finally

make up for childhood,
make the right one love you,
bring the dead to life.

Saturdays at the Met

Chet Baker, egomaniacal
heroin-wracked wastrel,
born trumpeter and con artist,
singing "Almost Blue" and almost
making it. And Astaire,
not the impeccable dancer
but the imperfect singer—
"Heaven, I'm in heaven"—
his weak, sweet voice suggesting
willed elegance in a depressed world:
approximating. Or latter-day
Lady Day, ravaged, hopeless,
yet all style. The many others,
nonmusical: Diana Vreeland,
a homely woman, insisting
to the last detail—even
to polish on the soles of her shoes—
on a private, abstract beauty.

Or, during broadcasts from the Met,
my stepfather, intense
pessimist and sometime cantor,
waiting for the high note,
squinting, his face compressed
with empathic strain, stubby finger
pointing upward, indicating

for us—the adopted daughters
he could not risk taking
to heart as his own—just what
the lyric tenor ought to do.
Ideal fatherhood suggested,
but impossible to carry through.
It's not the accomplished thing
that creates in others yearning,
but near-perfections,
evocations of the yet-to-be
and Promised Land: pointing to.

Blackmail

After writing of my dead stepfather,
telling small stories implicating
his unwitting or willful cruelties,
this dream: a wind sweeps into

my upstairs bedroom, almost lifting me off
the bed, then a powerful suction, a tug,
as it rushes away. This is felt as his visit
and departure. A longing pulls me after.

Now in the dream I'm downstairs, having heard
someone turning a key in a lock, maybe trying
to break into the house. My stepfather sits watching
a small black-and-white TV in the kitchen.

He asks mildly, each of us unafraid, unsurprised
by the other's presence: "But why
are you blackmailing me?"—in the dream meaning,
"Why are you keeping me here, in this life?"

Repeatedly attempting to get what I want
through what I know about him, like trying
a key in a lock, I have not let him be
through with failing to be what I want,

my father; I haven't let him go. Don't I also know
in his last months he stayed up alone, watching
TV without watching? Postponing
his heart surgery, waiting to die,

secretly, patiently. —And the wind,
that arrived without my coercion? Didn't
I feel him pulling, still holding on to me?
I admit it, the story was larger:

he had his own longings.

FOUR DREAM HOUSES   **t h r e e**

Big Sister

On the floor of her closet,
crushed milkshake containers,
Hershey wrappers, heaped
underwear and clothes.
That's when she's sixteen:
beautiful, enraged,
impossible to speak to
and flunking out of school—
then as now hungry,
dropping like laundry
the pieces of her life.
Divorced three times,
past forty, without
savings or job skills
and out of a job.
I'm forty myself in Ohio,
far from her California
rented room. Always,
when I call on her birthday
or New Year's, she tells me,
"Take care of yourself."
She doesn't phone or write.
Her eyes are not a pale,
vague blue like my eyes,
but unfaded morning-glory,
deep-lake-in-summer blue;

her downturned upper lip
curves strongly like a heart;
I hear she weighs over
two hundred pounds. Was it
I who kept her hungry
with my good-girl grades
and clarinet lessons, quick
words for her slow ones,
and for her early bloom
my safer, slower-growing
sex? Was it because of me
she swelled pregnant
and married at eighteen
a man our parents hated?
She rode in his red MG
to Albuquerque where he
beat her; when she phoned
crying, they wouldn't say
what happened or hand me
the receiver. My sister
in the backseat of the Dodge
where I stretched out napping,
my head on her lap; or
squabbling over Monopoly
or listening to *The Shadow*,
eating buttered saltines
as we lay on twin beds.
What happened to us,
what did I do, while
I was saving myself?
The stories families pass on
are crudely sentimental
but do know something true:
my sister as a toddler
helped Mother push my carriage,

at pauses in their walk
performing her ritual
of waving dimpled fingers
over my face. "Shoo fy,"
she repeated gravely,
working to take care
of the baby, "Shoo fy, shoo."

Blurry

The watery state I come from: dripping
from green to green, outlines wavering

in fog and rain; creatures guessed
at, screened by trees; and most

days overcast. The distant blackboard
in Miss Sodegrin's first grade—

where, anyway, I had
a fuzzy, vaguish notion, amid

peculiar smells (chalk and glue and urine)
and strange other children,

of what was going on. In
our fifties living room, my solemn

parents conducted an impromptu
"vision test"—among the chartreuse,

two-piece sectional, huge geisha posters,
green plaid wallpaper, stacked coasters

and ceramic ashtrays for their chain-smoked
cigarettes. They pointed and spoke

loudly, as to a foreigner, from the hazy
other end, "Can you see

this?" And I, "Of course I can." (If
the Lucky Strikes and Life

were blurry, I did know they were there:
Why take a chance on being, once more,

stupid?) But even with new plastic
glasses (red plaid, my mother's pick),

I still had trouble seeing, or
seeing my way clear.

Along the riverfront, on the way home
from Sunday school in rain,

peering at each tanker, tug, and barge
(through spattered windows of our Dodge)

and straining for the front-seat words
(murmured, half-overheard):

Our grandmother did what? They
"put him away"

where? How could she
"lose the baby"?

(Every day, more fresh confusion
on top of the old question;

about that, they wouldn't whisper.
Who was our other father?)

Their voices mixed with smells
of fishmeal, pine, and kaiser rolls

to chew with comics:
Nancy and Prince Valiant. Things mixed

and blurred. In my bookworm nook
under the window framing Mt. Hood's peak

(asleep between eruptions), stray
characters conversed, refusing to stay

put inside their plots
and spines. Left with connect-the-dots

and crosswords on stay-at-home sick
days, drifting in clouds of Vicks,

adventures of Helen Trent and Our Gal
Sunday, I thought the radio soaps were all

one daylong program, in which no one got better.
Degrees and decades later,

I try not to be stupid, but then get bored
or tired and drop my guard.

Most slips pass harmlessly,
and some are even funny:

"When Louis was on the phone"
instead of "on the throne."

Some acts are menacing:
blurting a secret out, or crossing

against the light. A good
thing I don't drive, but take the bus instead!

Inside this one,
it's sleepy, with snowflakes melting down

the window by my seat
in rivulets that meet

in tragi-comedy, as opposites slide
together: cowardice and courage, pride

and shame, tenderness and spite,
origins and ends. While outside light

grows dim, more pairs of things
converge: a building

and Mt. Hood. My daughter
and distant sister.

(Wasn't that our father
glimpsed at Gram's one summer

among forbidden photos?) *His* picture
and childhood's mythic cougar,

stretched out on a pine-tree
branch and staring back at me.

Stoplights and star clusters.
(In space, you see star colors

clearly, or so the cosmonauts
said: not twinkling whites

and yellows, but hard
blue, and green, and red.)

Four Dream Houses

I

The first was blue inside,
a sort of crumbling, tender
blue adobe—benignly
enchanted, and ready to inhabit.
Its style was vaguely Spanish.
(I remember thinking
I would never furnish
a house with such heavy pieces,
but still, it's perfect.) Dark
banisters and softly
colored Zapotec rugs.
Happy, I almost wept.
The large apartment where
I actually live has blue
venetian blinds, a striped
Zapotec hanging. But this
was the one house
where it could *all* get done,
and almost without effort—
the body of work I would not
(I knew it in the dream)
ever in this life own.

2

I live in my mother's house;
I have to live there.
It's rustic, with large windows,
on a hill. It might be
pleasant, but isn't—
cluttered, in disrepair.
My mother then agrees
(reluctantly, angrily)
to fix up the shabby house.
She's cleaning and painting
furiously—and she's crazy.
She's painted everything blue:
counters, pots, and glasses,
even the unmade beds,
rumpled sheets and blankets.
In front of the house, my mother
(blue paint all over her)
is grinning terribly,
pointing a gun at my body.
I get the pistol and throw it
in a clump of nearby bushes
before I break away.

3

One night later, I dreamed
of a different departure.
In Oregon, in the woods,
this is the house of my childhood—
familiar, but slightly altered
and perfected. Small nooks,
a yellow pantry, curves,
and pretty moldings—
a sort of thirties cottage

(from the decade between
my mother's birth and mine),
with splashy, flowered
thirties wallpaper intact.
It would, I thought, just *fit* me
and I could work with ease.
I told my mother this
(she came and went in the dream),
but I could not get the house.
She said, "You can't afford it."

4

I'm in my adult life.
My lover's friends, a woman
and man who are also lovers,
redecorate our apartment—
wonderfully, playfully.
I've come back after a trip
to find the white bedroom
is Pompeiian red,
with patterns of grapes and leaves;
the living-room fireplace
is now a soft moss-green,
with gold rococo trim.
On the walls are small and perfect
copies of Old Masters—
one a copy of a painting
that copied other Masters.
With my permission,
everything goes on changing,
sumptuous textures and colors.
When I wake up
in the familiar room,
in my everyday body,
I have a sinus headache,

but feel alert, like working.
On the white walls,
where for now I've hung them,
are prints of the Old Masters.

To Gram at Ninety

Rain falls on fallen rain, pocking
the clear surfaces it has made—each drop sending
out rings like the orbits
of the nine planets,
or (in very slow motion)
the repercussions
of a kiss given seventy years ago.
Playing a grand but invisible piano,
it will suddenly stop
without your noticing when the last drop
fell—like a lover
whose last embrace you cannot remember,
embedded as it was in the natural order.
I am not the first to say
it is all colors and no color—the way
a dead person you love is everywhere
and yet nowhere.
Or it's Time—that prince
who lavished jewels, now relentless,
the dispenser of pain.
See how, whatever its changes, the rain
is a cage you
can walk through.

Gram

1896–1990

I

Conscious of her beauty, unconscious
of her cruelties, a woman of vigor
and inescapable charm.

Who ruled her family
as her luxuriant garden—each life
a struggle for favor, the sun's touch.

Over her children, autocratically
watchful (no chocolates or white
bread, enforced runs on the beach

in all weather before breakfast),
and yet casual in her affections,
with the inadvertent

coldness of artists
or, like her, the self-absorbed.
From her California garden, though,

there was plum cake for her grandchildren,
whom she let comb and braid
her long, thick, bleached-blonde hair.

Her inner life unknown to anyone—
what did it feel like
to outlive two children, the third

of four daughters and the youngest,
her only son? Outlasting her yielding
husband whose heart stopped

at ninety: in that moment
he was reading to her, still focused
on her. For years

he'd accepted her sudden,
unaccountable flights—
a note with some cooked food:

gone camping with the children
(who, glad or not, had no say
in the matter); or later,

gone for weeks
to Palm Springs and her trailer
in the desert, alone.

2

Now we stand huddled
around this bed as if around a fire.
On the monitor a line,

a green abstraction
of the way her heart flutters
beneath the hospital sheet

like wings of a fledgling—
pausing, practicing
flight, pausing.

Once she says, to no one, "Cold,
my feet are cold." I stroke
her feet, say, "It's all right.

Do you want to sleep?
You can sleep."
And when she wakes briefly,

to a nurse or grandchild,
to any daughter, automatically
an impersonal, beatific smile.

3
Now, whatever they still need
from her, her three daughters
all past sixty, is beyond

remediation, permanent needs—
hurts that will press out
in large or petty ways,

as my hunger as a daughter
drives me. The next morning
her skin, bronzed throughout

my childhood, warm and pink
just hours before, is yellowed
and cool, resistant to touch.

Divorce, a Letter to Canada

for Yves, Spring 1982

I woke to your voice,
murmuring on tape to your stepdaughter
in the next room, and the singing
of two birds, unidentified. It's spring,
and the maple I noted last fall, as "a fire
looking for anything to burn," blows
small bells with many clappers on the grass.

Driving north in another fall,
a flock of birds shot
straight out from a tree together:
leaves falling up. We woke
each day together; each day
I was surprised to be your wife.

Mon mari, mon homme,
last week a man
looked at me over wine: my blood
flushed up, sudden as quail.
I'm tired of cigarettes, coffee, words;
of wanting—more tired of trying not to want.

We should be what we are not: together—
all the length of our limbs, desire;
the long length of the branches, blossoms.

Red Curtains

When I wake, I am forty.
Venetian blinds break the day
into stripes, dark and light,
across my studio floor.

I've lived in this country
and that one; married, unmarried.
Over and over, I've broken my life,
as a child breaks a toy

to see how it works. Outside,
white flowers sweep over
the fence. *Philadelphus*, Mock
Orange, but the stunned sweetness

they give the air is real.
Inside are these alternate stripes,
fragile strata of past lives.
Twenty years ago, dozing,

my left side confidingly against
my husband's young body,
red curtains rustling
in the early June breeze—

all that warm afternoon
their whispered insistence: *Impossible*
sweetness. And, *Isn't there*
something else, a hushed wish?

Lisa, Reading

There are other worlds and I have,
because it is a way I survive,
taught my daughter this.
She is reading *Little Women* on the couch
and I am reading the poems
of a compassionate, sad man.
In her book, four girls are waiting
to become women, as she herself
is waiting, reading about them.
Some, like Jo, will go to market:
they will buy what they will buy,
as I have bought this shelf of books,
as that man bought compassion
with his own pain. Some,
like Beth, will stay at home,
which is another name for the place
we come from and are afraid of
and long for. My daughter is thinking
she will be like Jo. She says,
"Jo wants to *do* things, like me."
I am thinking I am like the woman
at the zoo in the poem I am reading
who says, "change me, change me!"
And now I am thinking how reading,
like college, becomes for some
an endless preparation
for lives they will not live.

Look how my daughter, at ten,
looks intently at the page.
I am amazed at all this act
contains: how we clamor to become
while we drown in someone else's sea.
Not really drown. Staring at the page
all readers know, "Not me, not yet";
and yet, called to dinner or
the telephone, "This too is not myself,
not quite." So we might,
startled, say at any time:
"I am not here. This is not my life."

In this, our life,
my daughter and I hover
where all longing lies.
I watch her reach one volume,
then another, from the shelf,
and lose and find, and find
and lose herself—her lips
half-forming words while she sits here.

Summer before College

Berkeley, 1986

Since we've been to ballgames, I finally
noticed just last summer
how sweetgum trees are baseball-diamond green;
and because my daughter
would leave home soon, the long August sunsets
absorbed me like parting.

Late afternoon stratus spread out thick to
thin to disappearing—
sand strewn over a beach cabin floor;
then the sunlight lifting
a sheer, slow yellow curtain up buildings
(the low clouds now pastel,
too pretty, like unwound bolts of satin);
then the sentimental,
vaguely alcoholic display begins—
sangria, cabernet.
Grown maudlin (the whole sky now a wineglass),
a fond mother might say,
"Just the right mix of fruit, tannin, pepper . . . "
—but my daughter resists
such coyness, as the wide red sky cannot
be contained in short lists.
                              Besides, we fought: over
nothing, or always, in some way, about
sex—my imposed order

like a formal French garden of players,
the start of an inning
having to give way to errors, and grace.

Both of us lingering,
pulling sometimes away (the bay sky now
is almost accomplished,
sober), our desirable, difficult
parting stays unfinished—
unlike a long ballgame or a sunset
and more like the knowledge
she'll add to, reading what others have said
in classes at college;
like, too, my own repeated attempts to
say what it is I know.

Unlike Her

Then a day comes when
you're acutely aware
you don't know—haven't known,
really, for years—just where
the child is, who for so many
nights you tucked in.

At a job interview;
maybe in jeans driving through
another state, eating pie
at a diner; with a stranger
(to you, that is)—maybe
wearing nothing at all.

Whatever it is has nothing
to do with you. Everything.
Her social work competitively
close to your own job, fiercely
different; the pie intended
somehow to fill a hollow

you left; the stranger
reminding her of the man
you long ago divorced. Just as,
in a composed, antique-filled
apartment, purposefully
unlike your mother's brightly

cluttered, bohemian house,
you grip a pen, sip coffee
(black, though, like your mother's)
in fiercely unmotherly solitude,
putting words on paper (whereas she
would chat, words onto air),

and completing books—unlike *her,*
I want to say, gesturing at freedom,
though she too has been a teacher
with an overbearing mother
and with a face much like my own:
small and willful, determined.

Wishing to cancel for my daughter
the tasks I have handed on
is futile, wherever she is. And looking
at her hands or in the mirror,
any daughter, in any case,
knows where her mother is.

CRIMINAL DEFENSE   **four**

At the Artists' Colony: Lake Forest, Illinois

Everything is pretty beyond correction: fencing
of silver-weathered wood or stone, smothered
in ivy or honeysuckle, elms overarching

the road. Positioned just-so, in dramatically
huge yards, dogwood, redbud, apple
in blossom, and lilac in green-hearted leaf.

Everywhere—even the mowed grass along the shoulders—
a stunning, flawless green. Sunshine, but gently
cool, something like skin tasting mint.

On broad sidewalks, the shadows make perfect Japanese
paintings of branches, and every house an "estate"
behind those rows of gothic, groined trees

the cabdriver called a "cathedral." What do they pray
for in this town where, joking, we say they suffer
from "affluenza"? Of course, they must pray

like everyone—for love or forgiveness, someone's life.
But, as in the sunny coffeehouses of Berkeley, time
doesn't pass. Nothing's worn out, or looks new.

The street lamps and fences, are they *made* to look old?
In the quaint, weathered-brick local Walgreens
I bought what I needed: a cheap clock

for my temporary room. Walking back, surrounded
by birdsong, I closed my hand around
the disposable black rectangle of digital

time in my pocket. Tacit and smooth as a pebble
worn by surf, it keeps (and tells)
its secret while I wake, while I sleep.

The Shadow Plant

The plant etched on the wall sits in its pot
as calm as anything—
as any thing not

human. The cars sough by, less frequent than at day.
If I switched off the light
again, I'd see again how they

trace ghostlike, restless lights across the walls,
emblems of human hunger.
The old wood mantle-clock calls

someone, me, to task—more briskly than a heart.
The shadow clearly forms a parrot, perched
on the edge of the pot,

its head turned to the right—above it, on one side,
a stem with paired leaves stretching out like arms,
and on the other side

a single leaf shaped like a heart.
Composed and colorless,
it mocks what it is not.

The errorless bird is still,
having no need to stir or speak at all,
not being in need of a mate, or hungry, or real.

Autumn Drive

Ohio, 1988

Newly arrived in the Midwest
in mid-age, we drive under
pewter, lowering clouds
that presage an early
winter—past fields where dun
sparrows and occasional
rabbits glean; past wine trees,
copper, yellow, scarlet;
more walnuts, *Juglans*,
all in gold—exoticisms
almost shocking in the midst
of earnest houses, raked lawns,
pumpkins on the porch.

Different trees each season
move with their transformations
into the foreground, the way
members of each human
generation at different ages
come into relief. What was masked
by greenness now emerges:
following the first cold snap,
the delicate, sweet-butter-
colored ashes, the sudden
short-lived raging of
Euonymous, the burning bush.

But along the rain-pocked river,
the limbs of sycamores
are like mammoths' bones;
and there's a dead,
curled-up opossum
by the road. I'm tired
lately, so much of the time,
afraid I'll die without
having done what I intended—
just a body, just
one more unlucky beast.

Driving back to our still-strange
apartment, staring at red
taillights of cars,
dreamily in our own car
merging with that separately
yearning stream, passing
phone booths (blue-lit,
almost elegant), it seems
we could go anywhere
or call up anyone:
a never-to-be-born
beloved child, dead parent,
or still unmet close friend.

Tomorrow, in early dark,
in this life-not-condoned
that the neighbors think exotic,
we'll write again at separate,
hopeful desks; below mine,
out the window, ornamental
crab apples line the street—
small, round green
trees turning ruddy slowly,
ripening like fruit.

Fourth and Main

How many towns like this with streets of Cherry,
Maple, Church—or maybe, with a memory
of the East, called Prospect, Whittier, Salem?
Intact town squares with wedding-cake gazebos
and beaux-arts courthouses of sandstone, brick,
or rusticated limestone, their pastel towers
raised when commerce boomed, before or after
wars that culled the boys townspeople prayed for
in a multiplicity of churches—

What are we doing here at Fourth and Main?

Slim, with city clothes and hair, two women
in our forties they call "girls" ("Morning,
you girls looking for something special?"), or sometimes
"ladies" ("You ladies need a minute, or do
you want to order now?"), but in three years
of these Ohio day-trips, never "dykes"—
though one time in a cafe two men whispered,
snickered, and nudged each other. Oblivious
at first, taking their smirks for friendly smiles,
I asked the red-faced waitress what kinds of pie.
One walked out, saying: "Guess it takes all kinds."

Antique hunters, what do we hope to find?

Forties tablecloths with border prints
of tulips, teapots, berries; costume jewelry
—dress clips, earrings, bakelite bracelets great-aunts
might have worn; incised Depression glass
(amber, in the "Rose of Sharon" pattern).
All we buy goes farther back than childhood,
than our childhoods. If we choose carefully,
can we change some bit of history—find
ourselves possessed of relatives who owned
these things, and who, incredibly, have passed
them on to us, a couple like ourselves?

Collectibles for a dream habitation,

our world, separate from the larger one,
free of sneers and furnished to our liking.
For very little money, we'll found a country!
—What sort of country, though, without the other,
familiar one? Impoverished, too small?
A subset, then—like other private worlds,
needing, and needed by, one of the better
dreams among this country's many dreams:
that there be small-town streets named Plum and Cherry,
kitchen gardens, peace, fresh pie at *Sarah's,*
and even bungling, frightened men like those
who unsettled us in the cafe. All kinds.

Dream-View of Delft

in memory of Elizabeth Bishop

In Vermeer's "View of Delft,"
we down our dry manhattans,
our feet up comfortably
inside the seventeenth century
on plastic-webbed American
lawn loungers; we chat and smoke.

We are in the painting
without disturbing the painting,
drinking without alcoholism
or self-loathing. I'm not sure
what we're talking about—
this and that, relaxed.

We are together but separate,
the way the gold strand
in the left foreground
is a version of a shadow
of the gray cloud overhead:
foreboding seen as light—

or the way the sketchy two
female figures in the painting
stand almost but not touching,
dressed in dark blue. And too,
doubled, the red-brick Delfts,
one in, one out of water.

Everything is meeting
and not meeting in the dream,
or in the painting. You
whom I never met are dead,
and I was, just now, sleeping.
Sun inches up the red-brick

buildings here, Elizabeth.
And which Delft now is real?

Criminal Defense

The end of May. I'm up and walking by six,
maples arching to form a dense green tunnel
down the vacant street. My mind is empty—

or rather, full—overgrown with tangled angers
I scarcely understand, don't care to own.
You've felt this way before? Your life, I mean,

your *real* life, not being lived, and you don't know
whose fault it is? It must, after all, be someone's.
Two men, not young, low-voiced, next table over

at McDonald's, are intent on something:
"criminal defense"—and something about
a gun one of them carried (a hit man? police?).

"Unfinished business," I hear, and "twenty years."
Whatever else it means, their talk means pent-up
rage that finds some small release each time

one of them says "gun"—the way my thwarted
friend, a woman, too often mentions "bombs."
Of all the snarling rages flesh is heir to

(or that flesh *errs* to?), this one: in middle age,
waking after a bad night—sweating, amazed,
and dully angry (or is that *duly* angry?)—

wondering how it happened—what we've done
or haven't done, or had, and now might never.
Who stole from me, and when, that heart-whole future

I scented, standing, nose to the torn screen door
(I can still smell it!), protracted summer nights
at sixteen—yearning, feral, the music blaring—

staring at the white moon? Somehow it makes
a person want to fire a gun—at least
say words like "gun," or "bomb," or "snarling rages."

All of us here at McDonald's got up early,
walking or driving down the leafy tunnels.
We won't, most of us, shoot someone, ourselves—

and one or two might make up for lost time,
manage to settle some unfinished business.
How long have we got? Say, twenty years?

The Flood

Columbus, Ohio, July 1992

I ache from trying to save things: the floral
carpet, rolled up seconds ahead of rising
water, your brass and jadeite Deco lamp

and suede blue cowboy boots from San Francisco,
drawers of clothes, your books from the bottom shelf
(mostly Freud and Hardy). A motley picnic

lies spread on the living-room rug; a dreary
sort of first-story salvation. Behind
the basement-bedroom closet door, in cardboard

boxes we didn't find 'til hours later,
other, doomed possessions wicked up water.
Old Masters prints, your college yearbook, my

grandfather's *siddur*. Stopped twelve years ago,
my stepfather's voice, silenced once again
on soggy tapes; photos of your lovers

before me. Records of those lost to death,
lost to other lives—bagged now, out back,
waiting for collection. "It's only my life,"

you said wryly, discarding one by one
limp envelopes. And I thought that you must
mean more than just those dripping photographs

and papers: your life, like mine, spent attempting
exact records. Why do we make more useless,
sodden *stuff?* The body of work and the other,

fleshly body. I'm sick to death of mine:
publish, feed, and *love me,* they both whine.
And now, to add to the mess, I'm writing *this.*

Wouldn't it be better—cleaner, smarter—
to sweep a Zen garden of rocks, grow lean
on minute portions of rice, and maintain silence?

But others besides us lug things from the depths
as a claim to consciousness or a past:
cannon from sunken sixteenth-century hulks,

Etruscan drinking vessels, Roman pots,
bombastic portraits from hidden Nazi bunkers;
or dreams and phobias, repressed desires.

We salvage memories now. These photographs:
your sister, tall, laughing under a palm;
my great-grandmother, just out of the ghetto;

and look!—that's me—with unmarred teenage legs,
and my daughter at birth, eyes shut against
the labor that she, too, will have to choose.

Over and over down and up the stairs,
hauling out of the muck another load,
and another: for dumb love, aching all over.

Journal Entry, WordPerfect 5.1

Last week I treated two young friends to pizza
—banana-pepper, black olive—in exchange
for doing laundry at their house. We played
a word game—dice, a spinner, stacks of cards.
One card's directions: list nicknames, endearments.
(A timer, the kind Mother used for eggs,
limits turns and comes with the boxed game.)
My friends wrote: Big Red, Short Stuff, Skooter, Babe.
I showed my age with Angel, Sweetheart, Darling.

When chemo doesn't wipe her out, my darling
writes to save her life: a second novel,
lyrics to complete a planned collection.
I keep a journal of what else she does:
tells me about the other chemo patients,
their beautiful manners on the Barcaloungers;
from a rented video records the music
Voyager picked up approaching Saturn;
re-listened once to Tosca's "Vissi d'Arte";
watches with me the films of Preston Sturges.

Pausing to kiss the peach-fuzz on her head,
I bring Evian, yogurt, Sunday comics.

Last night, sick, she wanted a poached egg—
her specialty, not mine. I entered the kitchen
fervently determined: not an egg—
a moon, or world. And this is how you make it:
boil water in a saucepan. While it heats,
into a saucer, break an Amish egg.
When water comes to a rolling boil, remove
the pan from heat and slide in red-yolked egg.
Allow to sit at the bottom, undisturbed
for several seconds, until the eggwhite turns
opaque; next, gently, with a large spoon, swirl
the water (this makes an almost perfect, round
egg/world). Bring quickly back to boil and then
scoop out the poached egg with a slotted spoon.
Place it on unbuttered, whole-wheat toast.
(It's best to be fat-free when fighting cancer.)
Add fresh-ground pepper, salt, a side of juice,
and carry to your sweetheart or brave angel.

That once, when Price came to "perchè Signor?"
we turned to hide our tears from one another.
Outside opera, my love has never asked.
The only moon I gave her was an egg;
my art today's a verse, this lap-top file
I'll exit soon: Feb18.93.
The software will prompt SAVE?, and I'll reply
(part foolish question, part instruction): Y

Sublunar

The new, wide-legged, soft-fabric pants, in taupe
or moss or blue; the perfect platforms for
my forties suit. Shopping, preoccupied

with trivia like this, when my love
is seriously ill? I feel ashamed.
And yet, the mind—why wouldn't it proceed,

no matter what, in its too-often mundane,
drifting, and inconsequential way?
Fashion is just one more obsessive symptom

—like my well-orchestrated seminar,
or even how the house must always gleam,
down to the stove rings and the bathroom chrome.

If something isn't right you try to fix it;
when Chance grips big things, you control the small.
And here's that tired, self-reflexive trope

the poet shaping print, a little god.
But I'm no kind of god, and anyway
I'd rather talk about the gaseous planets,

Jupiter and Saturn. Did you know
there's a swirling storm on Jupiter
three times as large as Earth? It shows up red.

And Saturn—that unlikely, distant beauty;
that banded, jukebox planet! The outer ring
is shaped by what they call shepherding moons,

one on each side, squeezing it thin. It wobbles
between the moons' imperfect orbits, as though
some awkward student's grade-school compass slipped.

So what am I saying? Everything wobbles?
Our tragedies are insignificant
when you consider universal storms?

And should the poem conclude with music, shopping
for rings, Neptune, or twin feet of a compass?
I don't know how to end it. My mind wanders,

then focuses on helpful, minute chores,
making the coffee, laundry, next week's meals
—then drifts again. The satellites and planets,

glowing with various colors in black space,
with names from ancient myth or Shakespeare's plays,
go about their rounds the way she goes

about her work: writing and revising,
indifferent to pain. Moons spin; lovers
love as best they can; a writer writes.

Blue Skies

The air is cool, birds clamor, and there is coffee.
We two long "to goon on pilgrimage" in the sky-blue

Civic, one Easter egg among the other Japanese
factory-fresh eggs out for a spin. It's too soon, though,

for a road trip, my love still weak after her chemo,
so this clean-testing morning we celebrate by reading

this and that, instead. In Antarctica, sugary-iridescent
in sunlight, the King penguins' bellies strangely resemble

old-fashioned, pulled taffy. In time past, in South Africa,
there lived a blue antelope, the *blaauwbock:* first mentioned

1719 by a European traveler; species exterminated 1799.
Let's drive, she calls over magazine pages, to Wisconsin,

Door County, named for Porte des Morts strait where two bodies
of water "converge in a crash of violent waves that long ago

caused the demise of hundreds of unwary seamen."
And so we will: a few months from now, visiting the Moravian

village of Ephraim, eating boiled potatoes and whitefish
at White Gull Inn by the blue glint of Death's Door.

Notes

"'The Lineaments of Gratified Desire'" (p. 9) takes its title from a quatrain by William Blake, "The Question Answered":

What is it men in women do require?
The lineaments of Gratified Desire.
What is it women do in men require?
The lineaments of Gratified Desire.
(Blake's Notebook, 1793)

"Lisa, Reading" (p. 48) alludes to Randall Jarrell. The quoted words "change me, change me!" appear in "The Woman at the Washington Zoo."